Date _____

Dear _____

_____

_____

_____

_____

_____

_____

From

HOPE *for*
Your HEART

ROY LESSIN

christian
art gifts

Contents

No one is stronger than the
violent person who is totally
dependent upon God.

"His compassions fail not.
They are new every morning:
great is Thy faithfulness."

~ Lamentations 3:22-23, KJV

Pathways of God's promises

Imagine a garden filled with pathways that beautifully wind in every direction. As you begin to walk about you discover that no matter which path you follow you come across an endless variety of magnificent flowers with vibrant colors and breathtaking fragrances.

Each time you take a new turn your view becomes more splendid than the last, totally captivating your heart and thoughts, as it fills your soul with unspeakable pleasures.

In a similar way, the promises of God are the pathways that lead you into the beauty and the splendor of His faithfulness.

As we continue to walk by faith in the things that God has prepared for us, the beauty of His ways and the sweet fragrance of His goodness overwhelm our hearts with joy and great delight.

"For as the earth
bringeth forth her bud,
and as the garden
causeth the things that are
sown in it to spring forth;
so the Lord GOD will cause
righteousness and
praise to spring forth."

~ Isaiah 61:11, KJV

As a gardener faithfully cares
and tends to his garden
so that it will flourish and grow,
so the Lord will care for you.

God, the faithful Gardener

"Their soul shall be as a watered garden ... "
~ Jeremiah 31:12, KJV

God is the faithful gardener of your heart.
He has not only planted the seeds of
His kingdom there, but He daily
tends it with care.
One day you may feel His loving hand
pulling weeds, on another day He may be
securing a tender new plant to a firm stake of
His truth, and on another day you may sense
new ground being tilled and prepared
for new seed.
Always, there will be the sunshine of His
presence, and the nourishment that comes
from the living waters that keep you
flourishing and fruitful.

"And the LORD shall guide
thee continually and
thou shalt be like
a watered garden, and
like a spring of water,
whose waters fail not."

~ Isaiah 58:11, KJV

New every day

Flowing out of His faithfulness,
love, and compassion,
God has something new
for you every day.
It may be a fresh provision
to meet a need,
a timely word of encouragement
to strengthen you,
a needed promise
to help build your faith,
a new understanding of His goodness,
or an answered prayer
that assures you
of His special care for your life.

God will not fail you

"Not a word failed of any good
*thing which the L*ORD *had spoken to*
the house of Israel. All came to pass."
~ Joshua 21:45, NKJV

Placing your life in the hands of a faithful
God means that His care is certain, sure,
unchangeable, steadfast, and true. He
will support you, uphold you, sustain
you, and provide for you. In no way and
at no time will He fail you. He cannot. He
will not. He is completely trustworthy.

"I will bow down toward Your
holy temple and will praise
Your name for Your love
and Your faithfulness, for You
have exalted above all things
Your name and Your word."

~ Psalm 138:2

Great is Thy faithfulness,
O God my Father,
There is no shadow
of turning with Thee;
Thou changest not,
Thy compassions they fail not;
As Thou hast been
Thou forever wilt be.
Great is Thy faithfulness!
Great is Thy faithfulness!
Morning by morning new mercies I see;
All I have needed
Thy hand hath provided –
Great is Thy faithfulness,
Lord, unto me!

~ Thomas O. Chisholm

"The LORD who remains
faithful forever."

~ Psalm 146:6

We never need to live
as though God was small,
His love distant,
or His power limited.

"O Lord, You are my God;
I will exalt You and praise
Your name, for in perfect
faithfulness You have
done marvelous things,
things planned long ago."

~ Isaiah 25:1

In Christ

You have in Christ a ...
- faithfulness that will never be lacking,
- love that will never be exhausted,
- rest that will never be disturbed,
- joy that will never be diminished,
- purity that will never be defiled,
- hope that will never be quenched.

"Righteousness will be
His belt and faithfulness
the sash around His waist."

~ Isaiah 11:5

I've never read in God's Word where
He ever told anybody, "Go easy!
I don't have very much. I have already
strained Myself giving to others."
~ John R. Rice

"Your kingdom is an everlasting
kingdom, and Your dominion endures
through all generations. The LORD
is faithful to all His promises and
loving toward all He has made."

~ Psalm 145:13

God is always faithful

God not only gives you exceeding great and precious promises, but He faithfully fulfills them in more ways than you could ask or think.

There are things He is working for your good that you may not understand or see clearly at this moment; there are promises He is fulfilling you may have thought He'd forgotten; there are prayers He is answering that you may have thought were requests that had been denied.

"Faithful is He that calleth
you, who also will do it."

~ 1 Thessalonians 5:24, KJV

You have been called
to a life that will testify
to the faithfulness of God.

"Know therefore that
the Lord thy God,
He is God, the faithful God,
which keepeth covenant
and mercy with them
that love Him and keep
His commandments
to a thousand generations."

~ Deuteronomy 7:9, KJV

I am only a little sparrow!
A bird of low degree;
my life, though very common,
the Lord still cares for me.
Though small,
we are never forgotten –
though weak,
we are never afraid.
For our faithful God keepeth
the lives
of the creatures He made.

~ Unknown

"In hope of eternal life,
which God, that cannot lie,
promised before
the world began."

~ Titus 1:2, KJV

Trust God

You can trust God
because of His character.
God cannot and would not
ever lie to you.
God has declared Himself faithful.
To live life without complete trust
in God for every detail
and need would be
another way of saying
that God is not
who He claims to be.

Jesus died for you

You can put all your trust
in the One who gave His life for you.
How do you know you are loved?
Jesus died for you!
How do you know you are cared for?
Jesus died for you!
How do you know God is faithful?
Jesus died for you!

"Let us hold fast the profession of our faith without wavering; for He is faithful that promised."

~ Hebrews 10:23, KJV

The One that you are trusting
for your eternal home
in heaven is the One
that you can trust
on your journey here on earth.

God will provide

God would not have made you
   if His arms could not embrace you ...
He would not have called you
   if His power could not enable you ...
He would not have led you
   if His presence could not keep you ...
He would not have gifted you
   if His hand could not bless you ...
He would not have told you to trust Him
   if He could not provide for you.

"He will cover you
with His feathers,
and under His wings
you will find refuge;
His faithfulness
will be your shield
and rampart."

~ Psalm 91:4

God's unchanging faithfulness

God has been faithful to you all of your life. Even through the years when your heart was turned away from Him, His heart remained turned toward you. His faithfulness to you today has not changed, and when you awake tomorrow, His faithfulness will be there too.

"The Lord, the Lord,
the compassionate and
gracious God, slow to
anger, abounding
in love and faithfulness."

~ Exodus 34:6

God is faithful
to you in little things,
in big things,
in all things –
He will provide.

More than enough

God abounds in faithfulness toward you. That means that His faithfulness is only measured by one standard – abundance!

It is a faithfulness of the highest quantity, the largest portion, the highest rank, and the finest quality.

It is a faithfulness that brings God's "more than enough" into your life.

"He is the Rock,
His works are perfect,
and all His ways are
just. A faithful God
who does no wrong,
upright and just is He."

~ Deuteronomy 32:4

The oriental shepherd
was always ahead of his sheep.
He was in front.
Any attempt upon them
had to take him into account.
Now, God is down in front.
He is in the tomorrows.
It is tomorrow
that fills men with dread.
But God is there already,
and all the tomorrows of our
life have to pass Him
before they can get to us.
~ F. B. Meyer

A sure future

We do not need to worry
about our future
because God is already there.
He has everything worked out,
because nothing
takes Him by surprise.

Because God cares

God is faithful to you because He speaks the truth, because He cares, because He has the power to perform what He has promised, and because He will not turn His attention away from you.

"O Lord God Almighty, who is like You? You are mighty, O Lord, and Your faithfulness surrounds You."

~ Psalm 89:8

God is faithful, look up.

God is faithful, don't give up.

God is faithful, hold on.

God is faithful, walk on.

God is faithful, keep on.

Keep on

God didn't give up on you when you were lost, and He will certainly not give up on you now that you are His.

"Trust in the LORD, and do good; so shalt thou dwell in the land, and verily thou shalt be fed. Delight thyself also in the LORD; and He shall give thee the desires of thine heart. Commit thy way unto the LORD; trust also in Him; and He shall bring it to pass ... Rest in the LORD, and wait patiently for Him."

~ Psalm 37:3-7, KJV